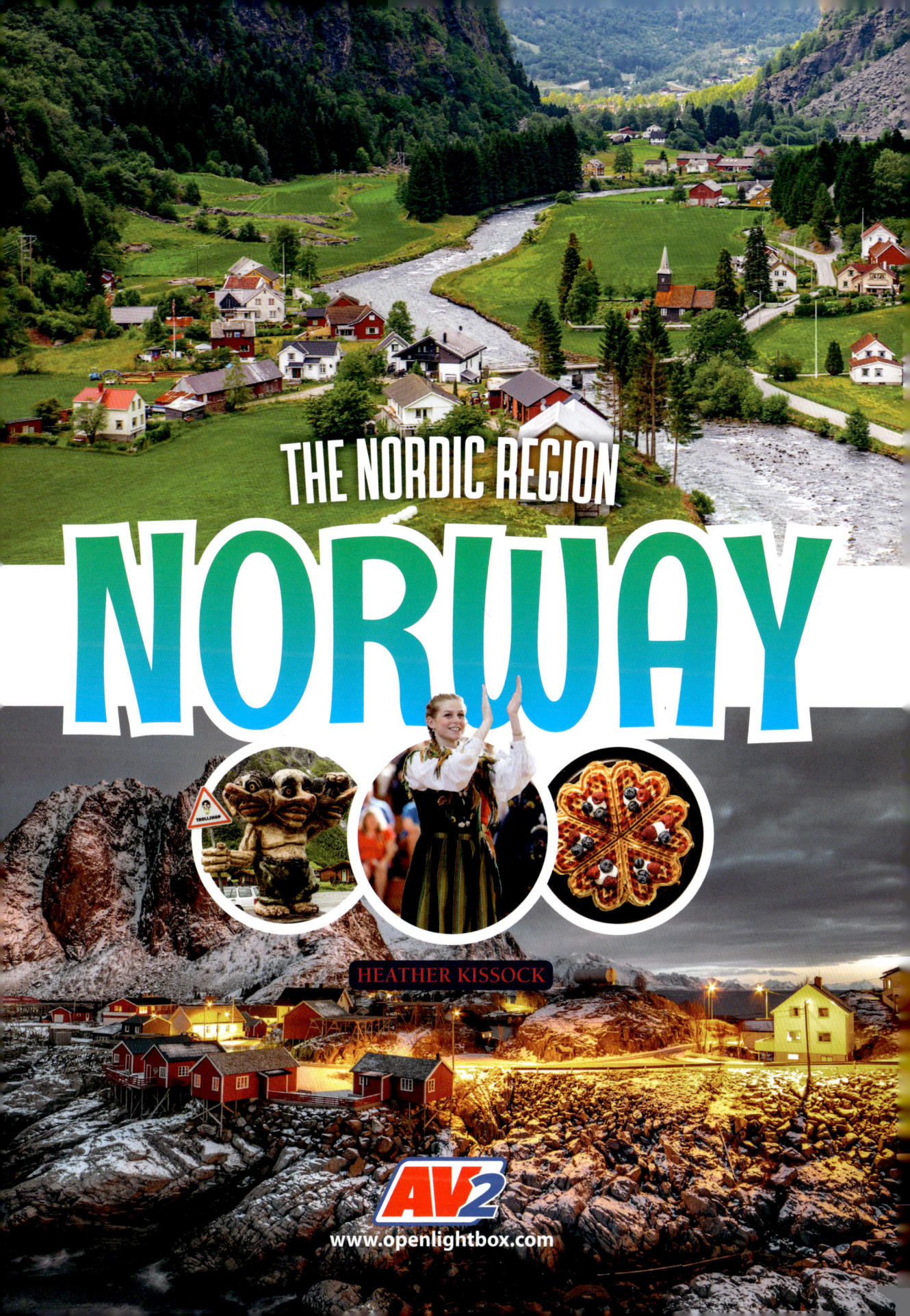

THE NORDIC REGION
NORWAY

HEATHER KISSOCK

AV2

www.openlightbox.com

Step 1
Go to www.openlightbox.com

Step 2
Enter this unique code

TXVRBT501

Step 3
Explore your interactive eBook!

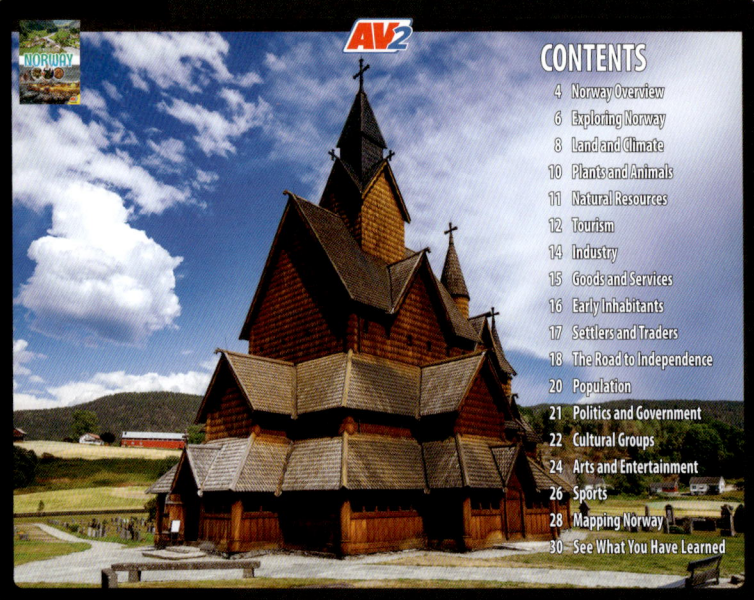

AV2 is optimized for use on any device

Your interactive eBook comes with...

Contents
Browse a live contents page to easily navigate through resources

Audio
Listen to sections of the book read aloud

Videos
Watch informative video clips

Weblinks
Gain additional information for research

Slideshows
View images and captions

Try This!
Complete activities and hands-on experiments

Key Words
Study vocabulary, and complete a matching word activity

Quizzes
Test your knowledge

Share
Share titles within your Learning Management System (LMS) or Library Circulation System

Citation
Create bibliographical references following APA, CMOS, and MLA styles

---

This title is part of our AV2 digital subscription

1-Year 3–8 Subscription
ISBN 978-1-7911-3306-1

Access hundreds of AV2 titles with our digital subscription.
Sign up for a FREE trial at www.openlightbox.com/trial

The digital components of this book are guaranteed to stay active for at least five years from the date of publication.

THE NORDIC REGION
NORWAY

Contents

AV2 Book Code 2	
Norway Overview 4	The Road to Independence 18
Exploring Norway 6	Population 20
Land and Climate 8	Politics and Government 21
Plants and Animals 10	Cultural Groups 22
Natural Resources 11	Arts and Entertainment 24
Tourism 12	Sports 26
Industry 14	Mapping Norway 28
Goods and Services 15	See What You Have Learned 30
Early Inhabitants 16	Key Words 31
Settlers and Traders 17	Index 31

Norway Overview

Majestic mountains, dramatic **fjords**, and crystal-blue lakes are what often come to mind when people hear the word "Norway." The country is definitely known for its scenic wonders, but there is more to Norway than its geography. Its past is filled with stories of adventurous **Vikings** and mythological creatures such as trolls and elves. Its artists and writers are world-renowned. Today's Norway is a progressive country with a booming economy, high standard of living, and warm, welcoming people. It has much to offer both its citizens and those who come to visit.

Focus on Norway

Capital
Oslo

Population
5.45 million

Currency
Norwegian krone

National Coat of Arms

National Flag

National Anthem
"Ja, vi elsker dette landet"
("Yes, we love this country")

National Animal
Lion

National Flower
Bergfrue

National Bird
White-Throated Dipper

Norway 5

Exploring Norway

Norway covers an area of 148,451 square miles (384,486 square kilometers). It is the westernmost country on Europe's Scandinavian **Peninsula**. Norway's coastline extends for 62,706 miles (100,915 km) and borders four different bodies of water. The Barents Sea lies to the north, while the Norwegian and North Seas sit along Norway's western coast. To the south is the Skagerrak Strait. The country's only land borders lie to the east. They are shared with Sweden, Finland, and Russia.

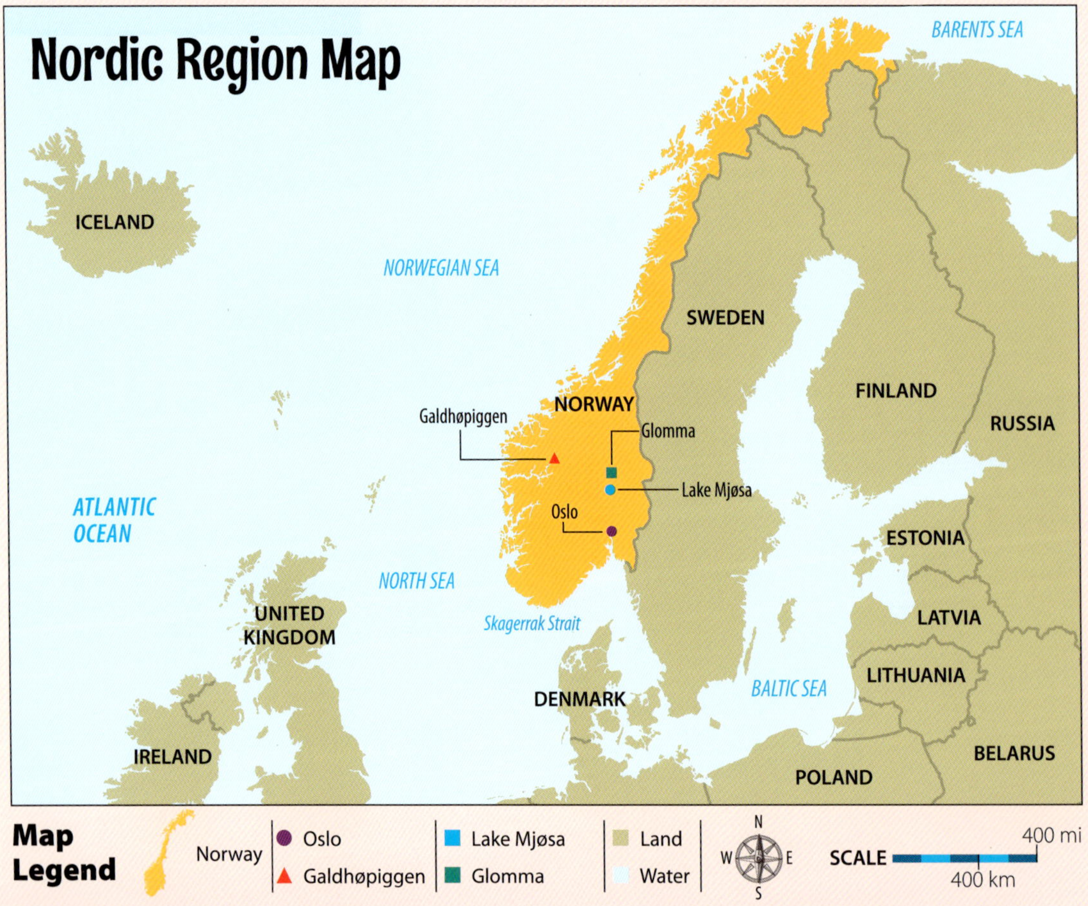

Nordic Region Map

Map Legend
- Norway
- ● Oslo
- ▲ Galdhøpiggen
- ■ Lake Mjøsa
- ■ Glomma
- Land
- Water

SCALE: 400 mi / 400 km

Oslo

Oslo is both Norway's capital and largest city. Approximately 700,000 people live there. Located at the head of the Oslo Fjord, it is a center for trade, tourism, and the arts.

Lake Mjøsa

Lake Mjøsa, Norway's largest lake, was created by **glaciers** millions of years ago. It covers an area of 142 square miles (368 sq. km). Many people come to Lake Mjøsa for its excellent fishing.

Glomma

Norway's longest river is the Glomma, or Glåma. It has a length of about 390 miles (628 km). The Glomma's **drainage basin** covers more than 13 percent of the country.

Galdhøpiggen

Galdhøpiggen is the highest mountain in all of northern Europe. It is 8,100 feet (2,469 meters) above sea level. Approximately 25,000 people hike to its summit every year.

Land and Climate

Norway is made up of five geographic regions. Nord-Norge is the northernmost region. It extends from Norway's midpoint to its far north, covering about 35 percent of the country. Most of this region is north of the Arctic Circle.

The Trøndelag Region stretches south of Nord-Norge. The defining landmark of this region is the Trondheims Fjord. It reaches approximately 80 miles (129 km) inland and forms the core of the region. Mountains make up much of the surrounding land.

Vestlandet covers the southwest part of Norway. This region is home to both the country's longest, deepest fjord and Europe's largest glacier. The Sognefjord measures 128 miles (206 km) long and 4,291 feet (1,308 m) deep. The Jostedal glacier, found in the region's northeast, covers an area of about 188 square miles (487 sq. km).

Nord-Norge is known for its midnight sun, a period in the summer when the Sun does not set for days at a time.

Østlandet has some of the highest mountains in Norway. In fact, Galdhøpiggen is found in this region. Galdhøpiggen is part of the Jotunheimen mountain range. These mountains act as an unofficial border between Vestlandet and Østlandet.

Sørlandet is located on Norway's southeast tip. It features lowlands along the coast and mountains inland. As the southernmost region in the country, Sørlandet is the warmest part of Norway.

Norway's climate is varied, depending on location. Coastal areas in the south have milder temperatures than the interior, typically staying above freezing throughout the year. Winters in the north and interior, on the other hand, can have temperatures of -40° Fahrenheit (-40° Celsius) or lower. Summer temperatures are mild throughout the country. Precipitation tends to be heavier in the west than the east. Western coastal areas receive about 90 inches (229 centimeters) annually. The east, on average, receives less than 30 inches (76 cm) of precipitation each year.

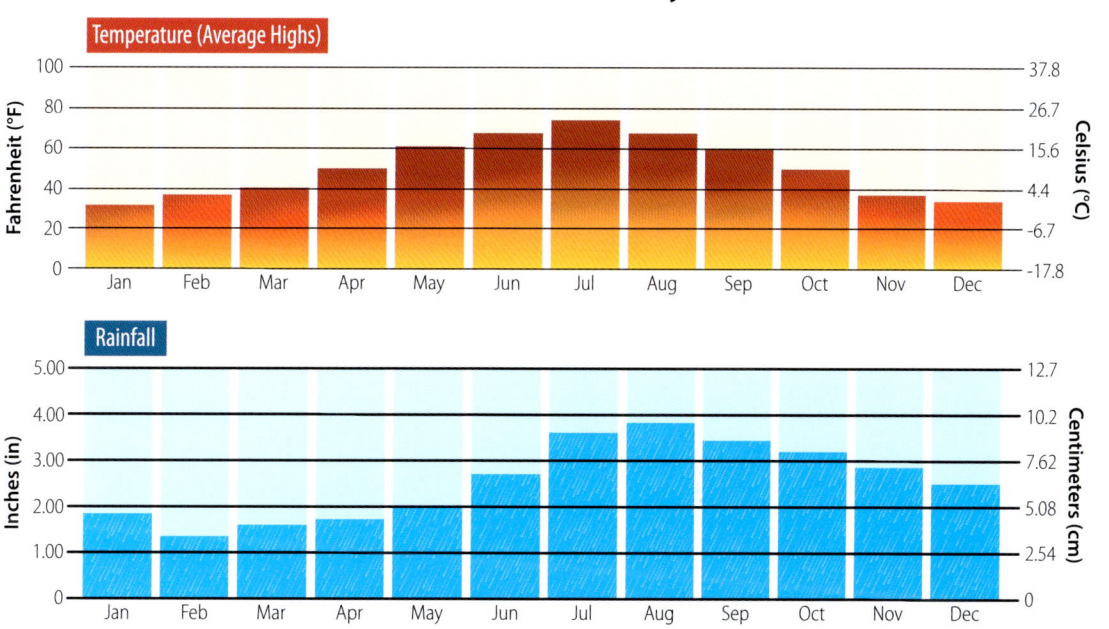

Seasonal Norway

Plants and Animals

Norway is heavily forested. Pine and spruce forests make up much of the tree cover in valleys. **Deciduous** trees, such as birch and aspen, grow on mountainsides below the **treeline**. Dwarf birches and other smaller bushes can be found at higher elevations.

Despite the harsh conditions, Norway's northern reaches are home to a variety of wildlife. Polar bears roam the coastal areas of the Svalbard archipelago, a group of islands in the Arctic Ocean, in search of seals to eat. Arctic foxes are common in **tundra** areas. Puffins can often be seen on rocky ledges along Norway's northern coasts. These birds are known for their orange and black beaks.

🇳🇴 The Norway spruce grows in the mountains of northern and central Europe. It can reach a height of 200 feet (61 m).

Wildlife is found in other parts of the country as well. Norway has about 275,000 reindeer, most of which live in **domesticated** herds. Muskoxen reside in mountainous areas, where they feed on moss, grass, and Arctic willow. Wolves live mainly in forests along the Swedish border. Beluga whales and orcas are often seen in the waters off Norway's coasts.

🇳🇴 The muskox was reintroduced to Norway in 1947 after becoming extinct in the country due to overhunting. Today, the country is home to approximately 235 muskoxen, all of which live in Dovrefjell National Park.

🇳🇴 Close to 30 percent of the world's Atlantic puffins have their breeding grounds in Norway.

Natural Resources

Water has long been one of Norway's most important natural resources. For centuries, Norwegian fishers have taken to the ocean to plumb its depths for seafood. Today, many continue the tradition of catching wild fish. In fact, Norway is the world's ninth-largest producer of wild-caught fish. The main fish caught are cod and herring.

The ocean has also provided Norway with its most lucrative **commodity**. In 1969, oil was discovered in the North Sea, off Norway's coast. Numerous oil and gas fields were found in the years that followed. Today, Norway produces about 2 million barrels of oil per day and is the world's third-largest **exporter** of natural gas.

The Zakarias Dam was built in 1968 to contain the waters of Zakariasvatnet, a lake in central Norway. The 2.5 billion cubic feet (71 million cubic meters) of water held back by the dam is used to power a nearby hydroelectric plant.

Norway's inland waters have made the country the seventh-largest producer of **hydropower** in the world. Norway has more than 20,000 lakes and numerous rivers. The movement of these waters through power plants creates enough electricity to power the entire country. Very little power has to be brought in from other places.

In 2022, Norway had 93 active oil fields. The majority were in the North Sea, with smaller operations in the Norwegian and Barents Seas.

Tourism

In an average year, Norway welcomes approximately 6 million international tourists. Many of these people come to see the country's stunning scenery. Some want to immerse themselves in Norwegian culture. Others are attracted to the country's Viking past.

A trip to Norway is not complete without a visit to the capital. Oslo is a thriving, modern city with much to offer its guests. Museum hoppers can view art at the city's National Museum, learn about Norway's seafaring past at the Norwegian Maritime Museum, and walk through 500 years of history at the open-air Norsk Folkemuseum. Tours of the Royal Palace, where Norway's current king and queen live, are also available.

Located in Norway's southwest, an area known as Fjord Norway features some of the country's best-known fjords, as well as high-flowing waterfalls and towering mountains. Visitors can cruise along the Sognefjord or ride a gondola to the top of Mount Hoven, at 3,317 feet (1,011 m) above sea level. People seeking more adventure can don ice cleats and hike through one of the area's massive glaciers.

The Lofoten Islands, on the northwest coast, are one of Norway's key destinations for nature lovers. The islands' dramatic peaks, white sand beaches, and diverse wildlife attract backpackers, kayakers, and even surfers. Located more than 100 miles (161 km) north of the Arctic Circle, the islands are also one of the best places in Norway to experience the midnight sun.

The gigantic Hunderfossen troll is almost 46 feet (14 m) tall and weighs 77 tons (70 metric tons).

Many visitors to Norway enjoy driving along the Atlantic Ocean Road. This 5.2-mile (8.4-km) stretch of highway runs along Norway's Atlantic coast and presents stunning coastal vistas to those who take it.

Although Vikings are very much in Norway's past, the romance of their lives continues to draw tourists to the country. Recreations of Viking villages can be found throughout Norway. One of the best-known is the Njardarheimr Viking Village, in Gudvangen. Guests can explore traditional buildings and watch reenactors demonstrate how Vikings lived 1,000 years ago.

For those who want to interact with Norway's mythological creatures, Lillehammer's Hunderfossen Family Park is the place to go. This amusement park is themed around Norwegian folklore. From the giant troll that guards the entrance to rides with fairy-tale themes, Hunderfossen creates a magical world for both the young and young at heart.

Industry

In 2021, Norway's **gross domestic product (GDP)** was more than $482 billion. The oil and gas industry is the largest contributor to the Norwegian economy. It accounts for about 14 percent of the GDP. Norway's manufacturing sector has also benefitted from this industry. The country is a world leader in the production of oil and gas equipment such as drilling platforms and support ships.

Norway's fish farms produce more than 1 million salmon annually.

Wild-caught fisheries still bring in much of Norway's annual catch. However, the country also has a growing **aquaculture** industry. In 2021, Norway's seafood exports were almost evenly divided between wild-caught and farmed. Norway is the world's largest producer of farmed salmon.

Agriculture and forestry are smaller industries in Norway. The country currently has about 38,000 farms. Most farmers raise livestock. To supplement their farming income, many farmers also work in forestry. With more than 33,000 square miles (85,000 sq. km) of usable forests, lumber and wood products make up about 11 percent of Norway's exports.

Norway GDP by Sector

While Norway's industries contribute significantly to the country's GDP, the sectors that contribute the most to Norway's GDP are service-related. These are industries that provide a service instead of goods.

57.7%
Services

40.8%
Industry

1.5%
Agriculture

14 The Nordic Region

Goods and Services

Norway exports its products to countries around the world. In 2021, the country shipped out approximately $160 billion worth of goods. Petroleum products made up the bulk of these exports, with fresh fish and metals following closely behind. Almost 90 percent of these goods were shipped to other European countries. The United Kingdom and Germany received the largest shares.

Oslo Gardermoen is Norway's largest airport, serving more than 9 million passengers annually. Most tourists flying into the country arrive at this airport.

Europe is also the source of most of Norway's **imports**. It supplies about 63 percent of all incoming goods. Vehicles, machinery, and refined petroleum are Norway's top imports. In 2021, Norway brought close to $100 billion worth of goods into the country.

Tourism is Norway's main service industry. It accounts for about 5 percent of the GDP. In 2020 alone, tourism brought in approximately $2.2 billion. The tourism industry also employs about 7 percent of the country's workforce.

Norway's coastline is ideal for shipping goods by sea. The country has more than 40 cargo ports, including the Port of Moss, a facility located on the eastern shore of the Oslo Fjord.

Early Inhabitants

Rocks along the coast of the Atla Fjord, in Norway's far north, bear paintings dating back to about 4200 BC. Many of the images focus on a lifestyle that centered around hunting and fishing.

The first people to live in what is now Norway arrived sometime between 11,000 and 8000 BC, after the last **Ice Age**. They are thought to have come from the areas now known as Denmark and Germany. A seafaring people, they were in search of new fishing and hunting grounds. While the ice had not yet disappeared from inland areas, the **Gulf Stream** had made Norway's coastline livable. It was here that these people formed small settlements.

About 1,000 years after the seafarers landed on Norway's coast, another group arrived. These people are thought to have come from east of the Baltic Sea, possibly from what is now Russia. They traveled over land, moving down the Norwegian Atlantic coast. **Nomadic** people, they were following the animals they needed to survive.

At some point, the two groups met and formed a friendly relationship. **Archaeologists** have found evidence that they shared their knowledge of hunting, fishing, and boating with each other. The nomads learned to fish and hunt seals, while the seafarers gained access to new types of tools.

Early inhabitants of what is now Norway are believed to have lived in pit houses. Built into the ground, these houses were initially covered with a tent-like structure made of animal skins. Over time, other materials, including rock and turf, were used instead.

Settlers and Traders

For many years, hunting and fishing remained the way of life for the people of Norway. However, in about 2500 BC, another group of people arrived and settled on the east side of the country. These people were farmers. Finding the land in the area to be **fertile**, they began growing crops and raising livestock. It was not long before the practice of farming extended toward the coast.

As more people moved to the area, settlements began to develop. Most were made up of family groups, or clans. Each clan was led by a chieftain. It was the chieftain's job to make sure the clan was kept safe from outside threats.

Norway's first written alphabet used letters called runes. It is believed that the creation of the runic alphabet was influenced by the Latin alphabet of the Romans.

By the 1st century AD, the Norwegians had developed trade relations with the **Gauls**. At the time, the Gauls were under the control of the **Roman Empire**. Roman culture deeply influenced the Norwegians. They encountered **literacy** for the first time and were able to develop their own alphabet as a result. When the Roman Empire fell in 476 AD, Norway became a target for tribes from the south. Forts were attacked, and farms were pillaged. The role of the chieftains became more important as more people turned to them for protection.

The Sámi people have lived in Norway for thousands of years. While settlements were being built in southern Norway, the Sámi inhabited the northern part of the country, where they lived in relative isolation from the other groups.

The Road to Independence

As the chieftains rose in power, a form of government began to take shape. By the 9th century, disputes between clans were being settled by a *thing*, an assembly of local leaders. If the issue affected a wider area, larger assemblies called *lagtings* were held with leaders from all of the affected regions. It was through these assemblies that people began to establish the laws of the land.

As Norwegian society became more structured, its people sought to expand the country's influence to other lands. The 9th century was the beginning of Norway's Viking Age. Viking warriors set sail to find people and lands to conquer. Initially, their attention centered on islands in the North Atlantic. Over time, they ventured farther afield, establishing settlements in Great Britain, Iceland, Greenland, and North America.

The Viking society began its decline around the mid-11th century. By this time, the Norwegian **monarchy** was fully established as a new system of government. Each king made his own contribution to Norway's development.

While the Vikings are known mainly for raiding and pillaging of other lands, most were also farmers, fishermen, craftsmen, and traders.

The late 13th century saw the country enter its Golden Age. This was a time of peace and expanding trade networks. The Golden Age came to an end with the arrival of the **Black Death** in 1349. This disease killed more than one third of Norway's population.

In 1380, King Olaf of Denmark inherited the Norwegian throne. Norway came under Danish control. The country remained a Danish holding into the 19th century. By this time, Norway's population was growing once again, as was its economy. People began to campaign for independence from Denmark.

In 1814, Norway established its own **constitution** in an effort to reclaim its independence. Only a few weeks after taking this step, Sweden invaded Norway and forced it into a union. The union was never strong, and in 1905, Norway was once again able to secure its independence. It has remained an independent country ever since.

🇳🇴 The Vikings were responsible for bringing the Christian religion to Norway. They built stave churches as their houses of worship. Today, approximately 28 of these elaborate wooden structures survive.

Population

Norway has a population of more than 5.4 million people. Most are found in the southern part of the country. Here, the climate is mild, and there is easy access to mainland Europe. Norway's population is considered urban. This means that most of its citizens live in or near large centers. Oslo has the largest **metropolitan area**. Combined with the city proper, it has a population of about 1.5 million. Bergen, Trondheim, and Stavanger are the only other cities with more than 100,000 people.

Norway has a relatively stable population. Its annual growth rate averages about 0.89 percent, meaning the population increases by about 50,000 each year. Births account for some of this growth, as does **immigration**. As of 2021, immigrants made up about 15 percent of Norway's population. Many have come from nearby countries, such as Sweden, Poland, and Lithuania. However, in recent years, some have arrived from as far away as Somalia, Pakistan, and Syria.

Bergen is Norway's second-largest city. About 270,000 people live in the city itself, with another 130,000 people residing in neighboring communities.

Norway Age Groups

Norway has an older population. The country's **median age** is 39.8, and the majority of its residents are over the age of 25. Norwegians have an average life expectancy of 82.5 years.

18%
Age 0–14 years

65%
Age 15–64 years

17%
Age 65+ years

Politics and Government

Norway is a constitutional monarchy. This means that a king or queen is the country's **head of state**. However, his or her power is limited by the nation's constitution. The actual governing of the country is the responsibility of three different branches.

The executive branch is made up of the monarch, the prime minister, and the *Statsråd*, or Council of State. The prime minister leads the entire government, while members of the Statsråd are responsible for running certain departments in the government, such as education and finance.

The *Storting*, or Parliament, is the government's **legislative** branch. Its main functions are to enact laws and approve the budget. Unlike some countries, Norway's Parliament is **unicameral**. It is made up of 169 seats, with its members representing the country's 19 **constituencies**.

The country's court system makes up the judicial branch of government. It is responsible for determining if the country's laws are being followed. There are three levels to the court system. The Høyesterett is Norway's highest court. It decides on any cases that could not be resolved by lower level courts.

Today, the role of the Norwegian monarch is largely ceremonial. One of King Harald's key responsibilities is to represent Norway at important events both within the country and abroad.

Norway's members of parliament meet in the Storting Chamber to discuss and debate issues. The chamber's seating is arranged in a semi-circle, with all members facing the Storting's president.

Norway 21

Cultural Groups

Most of Norway's citizens have Norwegian ancestry. This means they are related to the region's early settlers. However, Norway is not culturally **homogenous**. A Norwegian can be someone from several different cultural groups.

Approximately 60,000 Norwegians are Sámi. The Sámi's ancestors moved to Norway about 10,000 years ago. Originally hunters, they settled in what is now northern Norway. Here, they turned to herding reindeer to make a living. Today, Nord-Norge is home to most of the country's Sámi population. The Sámi are considered a distinct cultural group and are also known as **Indigenous** Norwegians.

Norway also has five national minorities. These are the Kvens, or Norwegian Finns, the Forest Finns, the Roma, the Taters, and the Jews. These groups have resided in Norway for more than 100 years. Each group has its own distinct culture. However, this was not always the case. In the past, the Norwegian government made efforts to **assimilate** these groups, along with the Sámi, into mainstream Norwegian culture. They were denied the right to speak their native languages and practice their cultural traditions. Recent years have seen steps taken to restore their cultural identities.

Norwegian is the country's official language. There are two forms of Norwegian. *Bokmål*, or Book Language, is the most common. Heavily influenced by the Danish language, Bokmål is used in most schools and for business purposes. *Nynorsk*, or New Norwegian, is spoken mainly in the interior and along the west coast. It is believed to have originated from a **rural dialect**.

Norwegian culture is on full display on Constitution Day. Held on May 17th every year, this national holiday celebrates the country's independence with parades and parties.

🇳🇴 Only a small percentage of Sámi continue the reindeer herding tradition today. Many work in the country's tourism industry, where they provide visitors with insight into the Sámi way of life.

Arts and Entertainment

Norway's arts scene is rich and diverse. Many of the country's creative artists are considered trailblazers in their respective fields. Their works can be viewed in art galleries, seen on stage, and heard in concert halls around the world.

One of Norway's most respected playwrights is Henrik Ibsen. Even though his plays were written in the 1800s, they continue to be performed in theaters across the globe. Ibsen was one of the first playwrights to pen plays about social issues. Two of his best-known works are *A Doll's House* and *Peer Gynt*.

Norway has produced numerous award-winning writers. Knut Hamsun, Sigrid Undset, and Bjørnstjerne Bjørnson have all been awarded the Nobel Prize for Literature. Jon Fosse, one of the country's most prolific writers and playwrights, has been a recipient of the International Ibsen Award, European Prize for Literature, and Norwegian Critics' Prize, among others.

Seeing examples of Norwegian visual arts can be as easy as taking a walk in the park. The country is known for its many open-air sculpture parks. Oslo's Vigelandsparken has more than 200 statues, all created by sculptor Gustav Vigeland. Stavenger's *Sverd I fjell*, or Swords in the Rock, consists of three giant swords plunged into the ground. Norway also has several world-class art museums. The Munch Museum, in Oslo, is a showcase for the works of Norwegian artist Edvard Munch. The Sami Center for Contemporary Art, in Karasjok, educates visitors about the art of the Sámi people.

Edvard Munch is best known for a series of paintings called *The Scream*.

Unveiled in 1983, the *Sverd I fjell* sculpture commemorates the Battle of Hafrsfjord, which took place in about 872 AD. At the end of this battle, Harald Hårfager claimed to be king of all Norway. He is still recognized as the first monarch of the country.

Norway's musicians have created music for almost every taste. Symphony orchestras around the world continue to play the classical works of Edvard Grieg. Mari Boine mixes jazz elements into traditional Sámi chanting songs. A-ha, one of the country's most successful pop groups, has sold more than 55 million records worldwide.

Several Norwegian performers have made their mark in films and television shows. Legendary actress Liv Ullmann was awarded an honorary Academy Award in 2022. Actor Kristofer Hivju played Tormund Giantsbane in *Game of Thrones*. Thorbjørn Harr gained international exposure as Jarl Borg in *Vikings*. Ingrid Bolsø Berdal played Armistice on *Westworld*.

Sports

In Norway, there is a saying that claims, "Norwegians are born with skis on their feet." Virtually all Norwegians have some skiing experience. The most popular form of skiing is cross-country. This sport can be either recreational or competitive. In fact, Norway is home to one of the oldest cross-country ski races in the world. First held in 1932, the Birkebeinerrennet takes skiers on a 34-mile (55-km) trek between Rena and Lillehammer.

Norwegians enjoy other skiing activities as well. The country has several world-class downhill ski resorts. Ski jumping and **biathlon** are also popular. Norway is home to the world's first ski jumping facility. Holmenkollbakken, near Oslo, started as a small recreational facility in 1892. It has since been rebuilt to host Olympic and World Championship competitions.

Norway is considered the all-time medal leader at the Winter Olympics, with a total count of 405. Most of these medals have come from cross-country skiing, speed skating, and biathlon. However, one of Norway's best-known Olympians did not compete in any of these events. Sonja Henie won gold medals in figure skating at the 1928, 1932, and 1936 Winter Olympics. Other legendary Norwegian Olympians include cross-country skiers Marit Bjørgen and Bjørn Dæhlie, with eight gold medals each, along with biathlon athlete Ole Einar Bjørndalen. With a total of 13 Olympic medals, Bjørndalen is known as the "King of Biathlon." Norway has hosted the Winter Olympics twice. The games were held in Oslo in 1952 and Lillehammer in 1994.

While much emphasis is placed on Norway's winter sports, the country also offers a wide range of summer sporting activities. Many Norwegians relax by hiking, kayaking, or fishing. For those wanting more excitement, the country offers a variety of extreme sports. Opportunities to go mountain biking, rock climbing, and whitewater rafting abound. When it comes to spectator sports, nothing surpasses the country's fascination with soccer. Norwegians turn out for its national team's games in droves.

🇳🇴 The Arctic Race of Norway brings cyclists from around the world. Together, they travel a route more than 375 miles (600 km) long, passing by some of northern Norway's most stunning scenery.

🇳🇴 Mats Zuccarello is considered the most successful hockey player to come out of Norway. He joined North America's National Hockey League in 2010 and currently plays with the Minnesota Wild.

Mapping Norway

We use many tools to interpret maps and to understand the locations of features such as cities, states, lakes, and rivers. The map below has many tools to help interpret information on the map of Norway.

Norway Map

MAP LEGEND

- ★ Capital City
- ● City
- ▭ Body of Water
- ╲ Longitude & Latitude
- ┄ Country Border
- ▲ Glacier
- ▭ Norway
- ▭ Other Countries

Mapping Tools

- The compass rose shows north, south, east, and west. The points in-between represent northeast, northwest, southeast, and southwest.

- The map scale shows that the distances on a map represent much longer distances in real life. If you measure the distance between objects on a map, you can use the map scale to calculate the actual distance in miles or kilometers between those two points.

- The lines of latitude and longitude are long lines that appear on maps. The lines of latitude run east to west and measure how far north or south of the equator a place is located. The lines of longitude run north to south and measure how far east or west of the Prime Meridian a place is located. A location on a map can be found by using the two numbers where latitude and longitude meet. This number is called a coordinate and is written using degrees and direction. For example, the city of Oslo would be found at 60°N and 11°E on a map.

Map It!

Using the map and the appropriate tools, complete the activities below.

Locating with latitude and longitude
1. Which body of water is located at 61°N and 11°E?
2. Which glacier is located at 62°N and 7°E?
3. Which islands are located at 69°N and 14°E?

Distances between points
4. Using the map scale and a ruler, calculate the approximate distance between Tromsø and Hammerfest.
5. Using the map scale and a ruler, calculate the approximate distance between Trondheim and Lillehammer.
6. Using the map scale and a ruler, calculate the approximate distance between Bergen and Stavanger.

ANSWERS 1. Lake Mjøsa 2. Jostedal glacier 3. Lofoten Islands 4. 130 miles (210 km) 5. 160 miles (257 km) 6. 100 miles (160 km)

See What You Have Learned

Test your knowledge of Norway by answering these questions.

1 What is the capital of Norway?

2 How long is the Glomma?

3 How many reindeer does Norway have?

4 Which industry is the largest single contributor to the Norwegian economy?

5 When did people first arrive in what is now Norway?

6 In what century did the Viking Age begin?

7 What form of government does Norway have?

8 Where do most of Norway's Sámi population live?

9 Who is the artist best-known for a series of paintings called *The Scream*?

10 As of 2022, how many medals has Norway won at the Winter Olympic Games in total?

ANSWERS
1. Oslo
2. 390 miles (628 km)
3. About 275,000
4. Oil and gas
5. Sometime between 11,000 and 8000 BC
6. 9th century
7. Constitutional monarchy
8. Nord-Norge
9. Edvard Munch
10. 405

Key Words

aquaculture: the farming of aquatic animals or plants
archaeologists: scientists who study ancient human life and activities by examining objects
assimilate: to make someone belong to a different culture
biathlon: a sport that involves both cross-country skiing and target shooting
Black Death: a disease that killed millions throughout Asia, Europe, and North Africa in the 1300s
commodity: a product that can be traded, bought, or sold
constituencies: official areas in a country that elect government representatives
constitution: a statement of the laws and principles of a nation
deciduous: trees that lose their leaves in autumn and grow new leaves in spring
domesticated: trained to live with or work for humans
drainage basin: an area from which all precipitation flows to a single stream or set of streams
exporter: a person or company that sells goods to other countries

fertile: referring to land that is suitable for growing crops
fjords: long, narrow inlets of the sea
Gauls: residents of ancient Gaul, a region in what is now France and Belgium
glaciers: slow-moving masses of ice
gross domestic product (GDP): the total value of goods and services produced in a country or area
Gulf Stream: a current of warm water that flows from the Caribbean region across the Atlantic Ocean to northern Europe
head of state: a country's highest-level government official
homogenous: of a similar kind
hydropower: energy produced from moving water
Ice Age: a long period of time when Earth's climate was especially cold
immigration: the process of coming to a new country to live and work
imports: goods brought in from other countries
indigenous: originating in a particular place
legislative: relating to a group of people that have the power to make or change laws in a country or area

literacy: the ability to read and write
median age: the age that divides a population into two numerically equal groups
metropolitan area: a major city, along with its suburbs and surrounding communities
monarchy: a form of government led by a king, queen, or similar ruler
nomadic: moving from one place to another
peninsula: an area of land surrounded by water on three sides
Roman Empire: the lands and people subject to the authority of ancient Rome between the 1st and 5th centuries AD
rural dialect: a form of language spoken by people outside of cities
treeline: the point on a mountain above which no trees can grow
tundra: treeless regions known for their cold climate and lack of precipitation
unicameral: having a single legislative house
Vikings: a group of warriors who raided and settled much of coastal Europe in the 9th and 10th centuries

Index

agriculture 14
animals 5, 10, 16
Arctic Circle 8, 12

chieftains 17, 18

Denmark 6, 16, 18

economy 4, 14, 18, 30

fishing 7, 11, 14, 15, 16, 17, 18, 26
fjords 4, 7, 8, 12, 15, 16, 25
forestry 14

Galdhøpiggen 6, 7, 8
glaciers 7, 8, 12, 28, 29
Glomma 6, 7, 30
Golden Age 18
government 18, 21, 22, 30
Grieg, Edvard 25

Ibsen, Henrik 24
immigrants 16, 20

Lake Mjøsa 6, 7, 28, 29
language 22
Lofoten Islands 12, 28, 29

midnight sun 8, 12
Munch, Edvard 24, 30
museums 12, 24

natural resources 11

oil and gas industry 11, 14, 30
Olympics 26, 30
Oslo 5, 6, 7, 12, 15, 20, 24, 26, 28, 29, 30

plants 10

Roman Empire 17

Sámi 17, 22, 23, 24, 25, 30
Scandinavian Peninsula 6
settlement 16, 17, 18, 22
skiing 26
Sweden 6, 19, 20, 28

Ullmann, Liv 25

Vikings 4, 12, 13, 18, 19, 30

Get the best of both worlds.

AV2 bridges the gap between print and digital.

The expandable resources toolbar enables quick access to content including **videos**, **audio**, **activities**, **weblinks**, **slideshows**, **quizzes**, and **key words**.

Animated videos make static images come alive.

Resource icons on each page help readers to further **explore key concepts**.

Published by Lightbox Learning Inc.
276 5th Avenue, Suite 704 #917
New York, NY 10001
Website: www.openlightbox.com

Copyright ©2024 Lightbox Learning Inc.
All rights reserved. No part of this publication may be reproduced, stored in a retrieval system, or transmitted in any form or by any means, electronic, mechanical, photocopying, recording, or otherwise, without the prior written permission of the publisher.

Library of Congress Control Number: 2022951617

ISBN 978-1-7911-4721-1 (hardcover)
ISBN 978-1-7911-4722-8 (softcover)
ISBN 978-1-7911-4723-5 (multi-user eBook)

Printed in Guangzhou, China
1 2 3 4 5 6 7 8 9 0 27 26 25 24 23

022023
101322

Project Coordinator Heather Kissock
Designer Terry Paulhus

Photo Credits
Every reasonable effort has been made to trace ownership and to obtain permission to reprint copyright material. The publisher would be pleased to have any errors or omissions brought to its attention so that they may be corrected in subsequent printings. The publisher acknowledges Alamy, Newscom, Bridgeman Images, Shutterstock, Dreamstime, and Wikimedia as its primary image suppliers for this title.